THE WAR BETWEEN THE

Vowels

AND THE

Consonants

PRISCILLA TURNER

Pictures by Whitney Turner

Farrar Straus Giroux
New York

Dedicated to all those Letters who perished
in the Great War

Text copyright © 1996 by Priscilla Turner
Pictures copyright © 1996 by Whitney Turner
All rights reserved
Published simultaneously in Canada by HarperCollins*CanadaLtd*
Color separations by Hong Kong Scanner Arts
Printed and bound in the United States of America
by Worzalla
Designed by Lilian Rosenstreich
First edition, 1996

Library of Congress Cataloging-in-Publication Data
Turner, Priscilla.
The war between the vowels and the consonants / Priscilla Turner ;
pictures by Whitney Turner.—1st ed.
p. cm.
[1. War—Fiction. 2. English language—Vowels—Fiction.
3. English language—Consonants—Fiction. 4. Alphabet—Fiction.]
I. Turner, Whitney, ill. II. Title.
PZ7.T8575War   1996   [E]—dc20   95-37587   CIP   AC

For as long as any letter could remember, Vowels and Consonants had been enemies.

Capital P's (which is what lowercase p's grow up to be) warned their children: "Never trust a Vowel! The long and short of it is, they are sly, cunning, two-faced creatures!"

And every little a, e, i, o, or u knew better than to stray into the Consonant Quarter. Who could imagine what horrible things a gang of roving Consonants might do to an unsuspecting Vowel?

The Vowels tended to be smug and stuck up. After all, there were fewer of them. Surely, they felt, that made them better than the common Consonants.

For their part, the Consonants thought all Vowels were sissies. "Those silly Vowel sounds!" they would say, laughing to each other. "AAAA and UUUU—what sort of noise is that for a letter to make!" Consonants preferred their own sounds: PRGHT! or SSSSP! Good, strong, snapping noises.

Most of the time, the Consonants and the Vowels just disliked and distrusted each other.
But one day . . .

A taunt was answered with a rock . . .

The rock with a spear . . .

The spear with a catapult . . .
The catapult with . . .

WAR!

The Vowel admirals met at Battle Headquarters and planned their attack: "We'll hit them with our screeching sounds—surely they have no defense against I's before E's!"

At the same time, the Consonant generals were plotting their own strategy: "Let those barnyard sounds try to stop the snarling GRRR's."

The Y's were a house divided. Some fought for the Consonants and others for the Vowels. It was brother against brother, sister against sister, parent against child. Some Y's became spies.

All the hospitals were full and overflowing. Each day, hundreds of wounded letters limped or were carried to Red Cross stations.

But the letters
continued to fight.

On land, by sea,

And in the air.

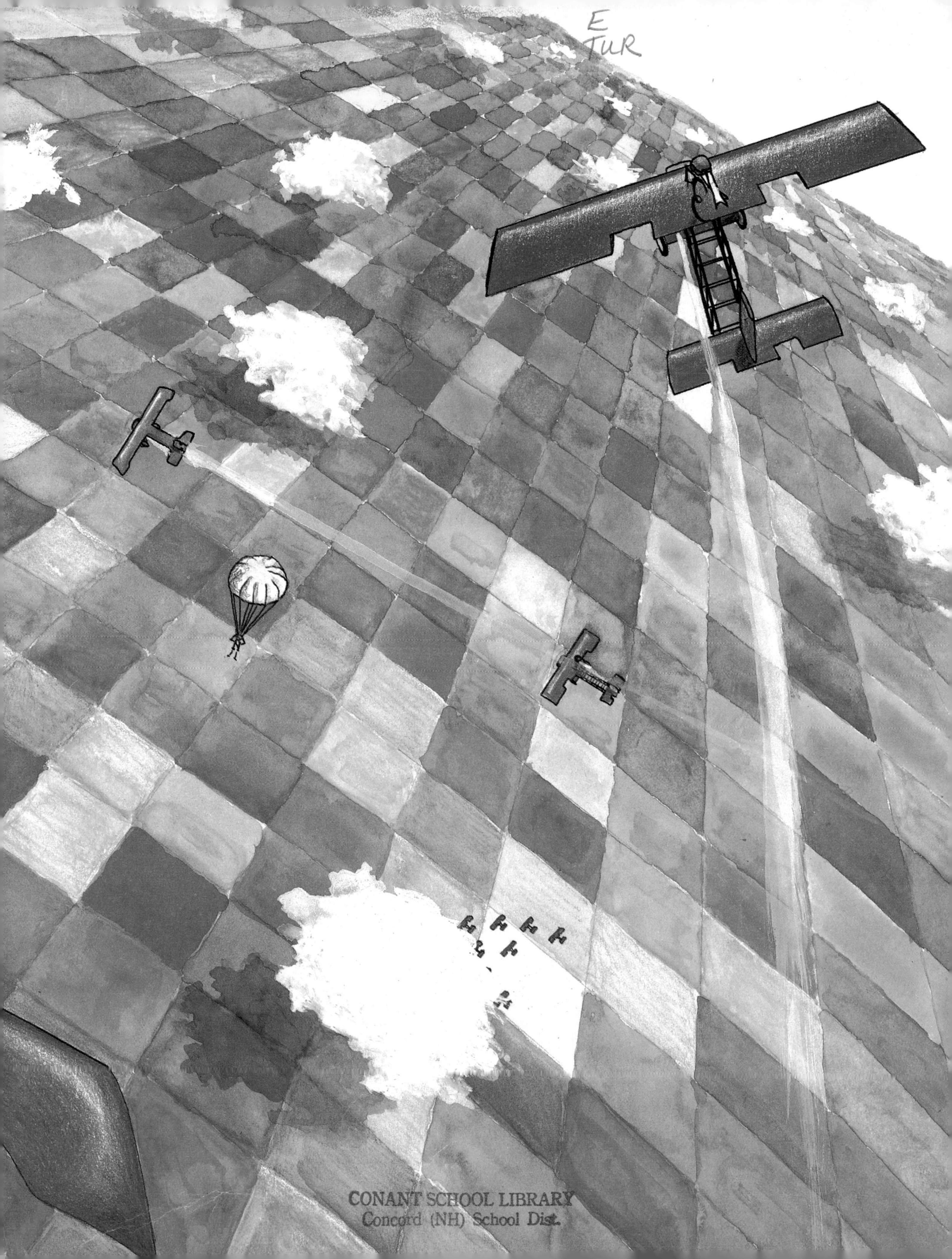

So involved were the letters in the battle that they didn't notice the huge cloud of dust peeking over the horizon.

Terrified scouts brought back reports of the senseless destruction left in its wake.

And then it was close enough to see. All the fighting
stopped as each side puzzled over the menacing intruder.

Great scrawling, scratching, scribbling,
horrible, sprawling, jarring chaos.

Fierce, wicked, scary lines and circles.
Zigs and zags with no form at all.

The Consonants charged first. Wave upon wave of their most fearsome combinations. The threatening walls of M's, N's, and W's. The snakelike S's. The freezing BR's.

Next came the Vowels . . . Shrieking letters dropped
from Vowelplanes.

"NOISE," sneered the evil scribble. "I'm not afraid of noise! Just try to stop me!"

The letters panicked.

All but one.

The youngest y interrupted the Supreme Command and the Commander in Chief and whispered something which only they could hear.

The commanders barked an order. Four brave letters marched forward.

The scratching backed away.
It turned around . . .
. . . but there was no escape.

Words! Sentences!
"I can't fight that," whimpered the jumble. "Next they'll make paragraphs . . . pages . . . chapters . . ."

The scrawl rolled out of town, no more threatening than a tangled ball of yarn.

The Supreme Command turned to the
Commander in Chief. "Just think what we
can accomplish together . . . The poems!
The plays! Our memoirs!"

Then they strolled back to the Supreme
Command's tent for a couple of truly
excellent chocolate cigars.